Secrets of Online Business Persuasion

How to generate more sales from your online business

By

Darren D O Connell

Contents

Chapter 1

Introduction to Improved Online Marketing Techniques

Anyone can learn how to market their products and services online – but it takes vision to see that those ahead of the curb are doing something different. In recent years online marketing has redefined the way we perceive the potential buying public. Those who have come to recognize the shift have profited from it, earning millions in online revenue by capitalizing on exclusive insider knowledge.

How did they do it?

The Evolution of Online Marketing

Let's get back to basics. A few years ago the Internet was different, a place where old sales techniques were applied in a completely new virtual arena. Slowly the entrepreneurs promoting online products realized that people were not responding well to the old pitches. Something had to change. Sales had to increase, but how?

By improving their online marketing techniques!

A new arena called for a fresh way to sell - and marketing evolved, branching out to reach the largest possible audience. Savvy marketers sought better ways to advertise, to present their products and to build a loyal client base. These needs still exist today in a fiercely competitive market. Make no mistake, without the proper use of every modern marketing technique at your disposal your product will become lost in a sea of clones.

How has the market changed?

The Internet has become a network of interlinking communities. Social media has tamed the once impersonal net enhancing the basic need for people to connect with each other.

Programs have been created that track success levels and analyze marketing data allowing you to actively and consistently monitor your progress. Competition for search engine ranking has quadrupled. This new Internet is run by public opinion, influenced by those in charge and manipulated by experts who use its interconnectivity to make or break sales campaigns.

Search Engine Marketing

Search engine marketing is a way to get your business more sales by using search engines like Google, Yahoo and Bing as advertising tools. The better ranking that your website can attain, the more people will come across your sales pitches.

Visibility is very important in online marketing – if potential clients are not exposed to your sales pitches then you will never sell anything. Through search engine optimization and correct keyword density inclusion in your website, text ranking can happen naturally. Advertising with Google Adwords or equivalent are your other exposure options.

These days' internet marketers have to optimize their websites on an ongoing basis as the search engines change their algorithms, for example when Google introduced their Penguin and Panda changes, sites that were on top started to fall. The sites owners had to adjust if they wanted to reach or maintain their ranking on the search results. These algorithms measure how relevant your website is and rank it accordingly. Because these prerequisites are constantly changing, optimization is an eternally evolving process.

Social Media Marketing

With the influx of social media comes the opportunity to market your business to many people, often targeting demographics or specific users who would be interested in your products/services. The social network boom can give your business that personal touch and generate a useful group of followers, who can then be marketed to directly via networks like Facebook ,Twitter, Linkedin and Pinterest.

Measuring Your Way to Success

Tracking your online marketing campaign these days has never been easier. With the rise of Google Analytics and a host of similar analysis programs like Stat Counter, you can track the progress of your marketing campaign from start to finish. Monitor how many visitors your website is getting, how many clicks your banner advert is receiving or how many people have read that promotional product blog.
See how popular your RSS feeds are, how your clients are responding to your email marketing campaign and how many friends are following you on Twitter by clicking on your business website. The integration of all of these traceable elements gives you the power to tweak, change and correct any marketing that is proving ineffective. It raises your success probability.

Many online marketers **simply refuse to put in the amount of time and effort** it takes to keep their campaigns successful. In an adaptable virtual world that is constantly changing, the clever marketer goes with the flow and sticks to what works.

The New Sales Strategies

You are just like those first online marketers, looking for a way to increase business and establish higher visitor to sale conversions. What fundamental skill gave them the power to create such compelling online marketing campaigns?

Why are their sales letters so effective and how do they attract so many people from the disorganized mass of passers by? Each of them knew that to sell effectively online they had to be persuasive, but not only that, they had to apply this persuasion to the largest potential client pool ever created –the Internet.

Every marketing campaign can be improved upon by implementing the rules of online business persuasion. This book will help to put you on a level playing field with marketers
who already know about the collective audience. You will also learn how to use this singular mind to create sales from a previously unreachable client base.

What is Online Business Persuasion?

Online Business persuasion in the context of online marketing, is the art of persuading a group of people via whatever means necessary, to buy your products, or avail of your services. In the past mass marketing has been called 'unfocussed' or 'general' and it was never very effective outside the online arena.

The Internet changed the idea that marketing to everyone was an ineffective practice. How is your online business supposed to know who their exact target market is? Better yet – how do you reach them on the Internet?

The old practice of targeting a specific need in a person has largely vanished. The power now lies with the buyer, not the seller. This is why search engines are so effective; they bring people looking for your services right to your sales page. Your job is not to find them - it's to persuade them to buy once they have found you.

Where Do You Apply Online Business Persuasion in a Marketing Campaign?

Your business message is a source of persuasion, your website, your sales pitches, even the amount of people who like your product factor into it. All of these features work together to convince your potential buyer to buy from you and not from somebody else.

Guiding a potential client to buy is a skill in itself. The important thing is that you learn to communicate to your clients in the most effective manner, so that they have **no reason not to buy** from your website.

There are many different persuasion techniques that can be used in online marketing. Once you understand group mentality you will begin to see how valuable the connected, interactive internet is to your business. There are no limits to your revenue sources, no restrictions on how many methods you can try until they work. The Internet is the perfect platform for threshing out exactly what people respond to best.

A strategic persuasion campaign will be the difference between $5,500 and $550,000 in the bank at the end of the financial year. By applying online business persuasion to all of your online marketing techniques you can have the definitive edge on your competition.

How Can Online Business Persuasion Lead to Marketing Success?

There are many different ways that online business persuasion can boost your sales. In the past, sales and marketing has earned itself a dishonest reputation. Many pitches are designed simply to sell by any means possible. This often meant inflating the quality of the product, exaggerating its uses, and making claims that are just downright lies.

People have learnt to be very wary of sales pitches because of this, and online sales are no exception. The fact that you can't handle the product or test the service is enough to dissuade most potential buyers. So what keeps them coming back?

The Networked Community

When an online company sells a great product it spreads like wildfire across a multitude of various network media. Your past clients become a future advertising opportunity.

This is because you are able to use the clients that were willing to take the risk and buy from you on faith, to generate far more sales. By using reviews, maintaining social networks, keeping in contact with direct email communication and by running an interactive blog – your customers will come to know you and in return, tell other people to buy from you.

Chapter 1 - Introduction to Improved Online Marketing Techniques

There are various techniques for gaining client trust - and these are an integral part of business persuasion. Building brand power, reliability and a solid reputation for your business will let people know that you have their best interests at heart. When trust is formed on such an intimate level they are more likely to believe your sales pitches.

Persuasion is so much more than guiding someone to believe in what you are selling. It's about establishing an honest image, a kind of symbiotic relationship between you and your client base. If your business pleases the masses, is reliable, credible and influential, then you will earn money. How much money you earn comes down to how much work you put in.

In this present marketing climate people want no nonsense sales from helpful people who aren't out to steal their money. If they don't believe that you're that business – then expect to lose all of your sales to the business that is.

Improve Your Chance at Success

In this book you will learn exactly how to implement business persuasion into your online marketing campaign. You will take a behind the scenes look at the psychology involved in persuasion and how it affects your business message. Then you will find out why social media has almost eclipsed paid advertising as a constant source of revenue for online businesses.

Along with these golden insider tips you will discover exactly how the 5 biggest internet marketers of our time achieved their fame and fortune, and how mirroring their methods can do the same for you.

Then we will go deeper into the very intricacies of using persuasion in every part of your campaign – from your website, your copy and your adverts to understanding the ethics involved with successful persuasion techniques.

Finally you will discover how to create and maintain the perfect online climate for sales and exactly what kind of influential tactics will put you ahead of the rest. By equipping yourself with this knowledge, you are putting your best foot forward in a slippery marketplace.

On this journey through new persuasive sales techniques you will also learn what to avoid, what damages your reputation and what clients do not respond to.

They are calling it 'interpersonal persuasion' and its here to stay. Think of it as something that has the reach of the mass media but is controlled by the people - no governmental or corporate force. Your customer base is no longer bound by demographic, language, country or time restraints – there are millions of people out there waiting to be reached, waiting to become a fan of your business.

Chapter 2

Power, Influence and the Psychology of Business Persuasion

Virtual Crowd Psychology

Many of the biggest online marketers will tell you that understanding your potential client base is the key to effective selling. In this sea of unlimited business opportunity where do you think your client base is located? This is a difficult question because it has no real answer. When you are selling online your client base could be anyone, anywhere.

This is why we apply psychology to online marketing. In order to direct your persuasive skills on your target audience, you must first truly understand who they are.

Think of the Internet as an arena, a place where people meet to trade at their convenience. Each shopper is part of something big, a massive potential client base milling around in disorder. We will call this client base the collective whole, and it includes every single person who may or may not want to buy from your business.

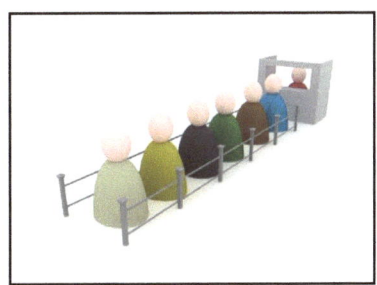

How do you establish the needs of the collective whole? How do you target them and get results? By applying **virtual crowd psychology**. When an individual becomes part of the collective, their attitudes, beliefs and motivations change.

This is because the individual is so influenced by the collective that they behave as the others do, and greatly rely on their peers to direct their actions. This is the fundamental reason that we are able to access our massive client base in online marketing.

The collective is susceptible to various persuasion methods that guide them to buy. These main methods include establishing brand power and becoming a market leader. They also include playing on your client's basic needs as a person who is also part of a large peer base. To reach the masses you need to learn a few psychologically persuasive techniques.

Real Brand Power

How many people are aware of the products/services that your business is selling? The answer should always be - not enough.

Establishing a powerful brand will help your business sales in more ways than one.

Brand identity online is enormously valuable – this is because people are drawn to companies that they have seen before, identify with, or that seem to have a wide reach. Brands are also associated with levels of likeability, quality and desirability. The bigger your brand, the more you can charge for products that have your brand stamped on it.

People love to pay for an image. When exploring brand identity – how do you think you can make your brand more desirable? Do you have a business philosophy or a unique perspective that could increase your chances of making that sale?

Brand Identity

Associations are a powerful way to persuade people to buy your products. Take a fairly new clothing brand like Ed Hardy for example. This brand has swept the world – it is incredibly popular – but why? The clothes are overpriced and they aren't that different from other brand free items.

Clothing designer Christian Audigier knew that he wasn't just selling a style; he was selling the urban street history that went with it. By basing his clothing range on a hardcore tattoo pioneer, marketing it as a young, trendy and yet extremely exclusive brand – he has made hundreds of millions. Think of how impressive that is – normal clothes sold purely on brand power - imagine what it can do for your business.

The lesson here can be applied online. If a group of people think that your brand is cool, of exceptional quality or the authority brand, then they will be more inclined to pay for it. We have all been programmed by the mass media to think that big brands mean the best products – use that ingrained psychological response to persuade people that your brand is best.

Visibility, Reliability and Image

Brand power begins with visibility. Investing in a recognizable corporate identity is the first step to realizing your potential. Nothing can be effective online if it is forgettable or hidden away somewhere on page 14 million on Google. How do you get your brand out there? There are platforms other than your business website that you can use to plaster the Internet with your product brand.

Social media networks are an excellent way to promote your brand identity and they're great for search engine optimization as well. Why not launch a viral marketing campaign on Youtube? Have a video advert made and post it there, before you know it people will be responding in new and exciting ways. Brand power is the key to social recognition and repetitive sales.

Become a Market Leader

Businesses that generate the most sales are always industry leaders, or industry "Rockstars" as Jeff Slayter and Kane Minkus teach. You need to increase the influence that you have online by becoming an authority in your field. The collective responds well to authority and is more likely to buy from a business that has a reputation as one of the best.

How Do I Expand My Online Influence?

As social as the Internet has become buyers are still wary about falling into the trap of buying a faulty product, paying for something that never arrives or worse, is of a really bad quality. When your business has authority many of these worries are eliminated right from the start.

By the simple virtue of being an influential business online, your client base has expanded and is more willing to buy. To expand your influence online and become a market leader there a few clear steps that you should take.

Quality Over Quantity – Every aspect of your business should ooze quality, from website design, copy creation, marketing and promotion to how you treat your clients. You can never be professional enough. Remember that reputation is everything in the online arena.

Know Your Business – This may sound obvious, but how many people involved with your business are highly knowledgeable about every aspect of it? Do they speak with customers? Make sure that you are constantly gaining positive feedback from your clients and that no negativity is slipping by unnoticed. Client feedback sections are great for this – make sure that you have one on your website.

As an expert you should be announcing yourself as one online, and creating a name for yourself associated with your business. Become a guest blogger on someone else's blog, or offer your educated opinion on industry issues in forums. This also helps when potential customers search your name on Google – all of your free input will be there for them to read – and you will be identified as an expert on the subject.

Use Other Media – A clean attractive product image can be enough to sell your product to the right buyer, so make sure that yours are up to scratch. Why not include some videos about your business? It will increase the interactivity of your business website and spice up your business to client relationship.

Industry Proof and Affiliation – This can't be stressed enough. People love to see proof that you are who you claim to be. Make sure that your website contains links, endorsements or affiliations to other leaders in your industry. If you have any prestigious awards or memberships then post them, they will only add to your influential status.

The collective whole is susceptible to this kind of influence because a group naturally identifies with an authority figure and adopts its belief system. This causes a ripple effect in online marketing whereby an individual will feel compelled to promote your business by word of mouth if you delivered on your promises. This will actively reinforce your market dominance and convince more people to buy from your brand.

The Psychology of Online Business Persuasion

Learning to use persuasion in your online marketing campaigns begins with a basic understanding of what reaches the collective psychologically and what doesn't. There are several important factors that you should implement into your business strategy to ensure that your sales potential is at its maximum level.

These are the basic needs of the masses that many, many businesses often overlook. If you are serious about making money you can't afford to get the basics wrong. Start by asking yourself a simple question.

What Do Online Shoppers Want From Your Business?

Convenience – This means a website shop front that works, a simple payment process and no hassles.

Guarantees – Do your products or services come with any kind of guarantee? Many clients will not buy a product that can't be returned.

Security – How do you protect your client's interests? Is your shipping method safe and are your credit card facilities protected? If a client feels like their bank account is going to be cleaned out then they won't buy from you.

Honesty – Don't make rash claims about your products or services because you will let your clients down, lose repeat business and ruin your reputation.

These may seem like obvious insights to the professional online marketer, but the absence of at least one of these needs is found on most business websites. Either they have a complicated navigation system to source products from, have no service guarantees or use tacky hard selling techniques to push their overrated products.

Be sure that your campaigns contain the basics and you will have effectively eliminated all the subconscious reasons why people shouldn't buy from you. You are already better than most other marketers online.

Time to Buy

Time is a very persuasive marketing tool that many pros use to move their products fast. Your potential client does not want feel like he has missed out on a great opportunity so he will buy your product. This is because it contained a simple temporal restriction that caused him anxiety.

This offer expires in 3 days.
Limited time only.

Psychologically the client feels compelled to act, knowing that he can't get that item in three days time for that excellent price. This is a great persuasive sales technique and can be used on almost anything.

Limited Stock

When a product contains the words '3 items remaining' or '1 left in stock' it causes two basic emotions in the potential client. The first is a sudden upsurge in the urgency to buy while there is still time, the second is a niggling fear that the item will be unattainable very soon. This persuasive sales technique uses the collective as a threat against the individual. There is of course almost always more stock available in most cases.

Independent Reviews

Social relevance is very important when considering persuasion in online marketing. The average individual is more inclined to believe another average individual, because they have nothing to gain from an honest review. The business has a vested interest in selling their products/services, so their arguments are less believable. This is why customer reviews, testimonials and best seller lists are so effective. People want to know what other people are buying and saying about your products because its more likely to be credible.

Be the Answer to the Question: Where Should I Buy?

The psychology of persuasion is not about forcing a potential client to buy your products. Remember that they have searched for you and are already in the market to buy most of the time. It's about delivering every good reason why they should choose your business to buy from, why you have something better to offer them than the norm.

If you can perfect the basics and begin to use the collective as a means of persuasion, then your online marketing campaign has more chance of being successful than others who dive in blindly.

Chapter 3

Group Mentality: Using Social Media to Dominate your Market

We have spoken in the previous chapters about group mentality and how each individual online is part of the collective whole that is internet society. What happens when millions of these people decide to converge on a single platform?

Social media has swept the virtual world and changed online selling forever. Imagine the power to nurture your own fan following for your business! To advertise consistently for free! To keep in touch with your clients directly, always engaging, always updating – it's a marketers dream.

This new kind of social grouping has allowed businesses like yours to grow exponentially in a very short time. Think of social media as the new gold rush – those that know about it want their share - those that don't, have no idea what they are missing.

A well planned social media campaign can take a tiny business and cast it into the limelight. It can force millions of people to sit up and take notice. This is why learning to dominate your niche market through social media is so vitally important.

What is Social Media?

Like many things online, a lot can be lost because of sloppy copywriters who spread the wrong information to every corner of the Internet. Because the idea of social media is still so new there has been a little confusion about what exactly falls under the broad term 'social media'.

Social media is about connecting with people, interacting, sharing ideas, information and media on a uniquely personal level. This can be done by using a social media platform. First and foremost social media is about interactivity. You are able to interact with other people, read their profiles and view their various offerings. You can comment on most things with social media – proving that feedback is one of the dominant driving forces behind the massive increase in websites that offer this level of interconnectivity.

Chapter 3

Group Mentality: Using Social Media to Dominate your Market

We already know that feedback is important in online marketing. This is what makes social media so valuable to businesses. By using these platforms and actively connecting with our client bases we can collect market research from an endless pool of sources, get feedback on products, be told if something isn't working – even receive help on ad campaigns from loyal followers.

Still not sure which websites are labeled as social media?
There are 5 main kinds of social media. They are:

Social Networks –
Facebook
Twitter
Bebo
Myspace
Profile driven websites mainly for communication between added friends.

Social Bookmarking –
Digg
Del.icio.us
Stumble Upon
Interactive way to navigate the internet and to save and share websites that you find interesting.

Social Multimedia –
Youtube
Pinterest
Flickr
Last.fm
Justin.tv
Sharing and commenting on videos, images, live casts and music.

Social Business Networking –
Linkedin
Xing
Biznik
Network with industry professionals.

Blogging –
Mashable,
Blogger,
Huffington Post.
A personal website that acts like a diary, personal collection of opinions, events, ideas.

Chapter 3

Group Mentality: Using Social Media to Dominate your Market

Launching a Basic Social Media Campaign

You have a business to promote and products to sell. Now that you know you need to launch a social media campaign, how do you go about doing it? In context there are hundreds of networks that you could join – but you want to target the most effective ones.

New business owners often get overexcited once they learn about the potential of social media. This results in the mass joining of 50 sites all at once. Your campaign will break down very quickly if you fall into this trap. One of the major pitfalls of social networking is that it is horribly time consuming and if you don't know how to attract a community it can be a long and tedious process.

So how do you create a successful social media campaign without wasting your time, money and effort? First of all keep your objectives in mind when choosing the right networks. One of your principle aims is to gain a community of people who will appreciate and interact with your business

From this group you will get clients, free promotion and healthy discussion. All the while you should keep in mind that this campaign must improve sales – one that doesn't is a failure.

You can have 4000 followers on Twitter but if you don't know how to generate income off them then the campaign has gone to waste. There are only two steps in the implementation and monetization of your social media campaign. Keeping it simple in the beginning and starting off small will help grow your business properly and minimize costs.

Step 1: Start a Blog

You already have a business website – the problem is that no one knows it exists. You need to stir up some interest in your products and services by launching your business blog. A blog does three things for your business:

1) It feeds new traffic to your business website because they are linked together. This in turn raises your search engine ranking on both of your sites, which equals more visibility online. A higher ranking means more people will be running into your persuasive sales techniques. You automatically get more sales.
2) It establishes a direct line of communication between you and your potential client base. Your reputation increases, your brand power grows as you give back to the community. Instantly higher sales conversions.
3) It earns you extra money. If your blog becomes popular you can sell the advertising space on your page. You can also use it consistently as a low cost promotional tool for your business.

How Do I Start My Own Blog?

A simple way to create a blog is from a Wordpress template. These can be customized to suit your preferred style. Wordpress is easy to learn and there are many online tutorials and Youtube videos that can teach you how to use it for free.

It's also a great content management system, and automatically organizes your content each time you post it. This is ideal for SEO as search engines like Google can better understand a website that has been well ordered. There is no point keyword optimizing your text when you have no structure to your website, the search engines will only see a fraction of the content that you optimized.

Great blogging is a sought after skill, but as long as you keep the content relevant, consistent and entertaining there is no need to worry – people will come. Add lively interactive features to keep people engaged - like videos, images, podcasts and music. Three posts a week will ensure that your blog never gets old or loses client interest.

Online Blogging

Having your own business blog is always a great idea but if you are not ready to cross over into owning yet another website, then you can use one of the free online blogging services.

These websites enable you to keep blogging about your business even though you don't have a domain of your own. Try Blogger, Tblog, Squidoo or Hubpages for great blogging platforms – they are all free and within minutes your first blog post can be published.

Don't forget to link your blog to your other social media!

Step 2: Join Facebook and Twitter

Facebook and Twitter in this instance will be used to draw targeted traffic to your blog site and eventually to your business sales pages. They are two of the biggest social media sites available and have millions of people who are members.

In essence, Facebook will be used as another source of advertising for your business but also as a place to create a following, to gain fans, to increase your status as an industry leader, expand the reach of your brand and to get active feedback from people seeing your business from an outside perspective.

Twitter on the other hand is used to promote your blog – any posts that you write can be linked to twitter and a tweet will let your followers know that something new is available to read. It's also a great place to advertise and let people know what your business is all about in a quick, friendly and conversational manner.

Both of these social media can be linked to each other and both can carry links from your business website and blog. You web presence will increase and your search engine ranking will improve.

Setting up Your Business Account on Facebook:

You need to have a personal profile in order to open a business account because the two are linked, so if you haven't got one yet you will have to start from scratch. Once this is done and you are signed in, go to the very bottom of the page and a click on the word 'advertising'.

At the top of the next page select the 'pages' option. Click 'create a page' and put your business page together. Be sure to upload a picture that fits the profile image dimensions or the thumbnail may come out wrong.

Facebook takes you through the rest in a logical sequence. You will need to add content, your business information, pictures, videos – anything that you think will enhance your business image and attract fans. Once you have clicked publish don't forget to invite your personal friends to join your business page!

Facebook also has an advertising service whereby you create a mini ad and then they circulate it around the network. You only pay when people click on it.

Tips and Hints:

For an effective Facebook page add unique content to the discussion section and stimulate some positive discussion about something relevant. Pictures and videos are more likely to be marketed virally if they are funny – why not create one with your business message? Add a reviews application so that people can give you feedback on your products or services.

Setting up Your Business Account on Twitter:

Sign up for a normal account on Twitter – there isn't a business option, but you can change your profile to indicate that it's for a business. Customize your Twitter page by writing an incredibly brief snippet about your business in the 'account' section of the settings page in one line bio.

Upload a high resolution tiny picture into your profile image. There are a lot of Twitter users who follow you based on whether your image is appealing or not. If you choose to go for a photo of yourself make sure it's a good one. This can be good for the personalization of your business.

Have a background image designed with your logo, a witty saying and perhaps a pic of you in it as well. When Twitter users visit your tweet page it must be interesting enough to read and attractive enough to look at. This is what will help retain the follows that you get.

Once your page is up and running use it to link to your blog, other websites of interest and your business sales page. Micro blogging is about giving as much back to the community as taking from it. If you spam people they will stop following you. If you give them interesting news, updates, cool website posts you found and so on – they will grow to respect you and join your Facebook page, read your blog and buy something.

Tips and Hints:

People who are interactive on Twitter and offer valuable microblogs are followed more often. Wit, personality and humor are king when writing your tweets. Don't post random quotes or funny sayings to get followers – everyone does it. Do keyword research to maximize your search potential. Your blog, Facebook and Twitter account handled well will prove to be a successful social media campaign and earn your business a lot of additional revenue.

Keeping up to date on what works best on social media platforms will give your business the edge. Each has a formula to be cracked – and it may take some time, but once you've done it the rewards are endless. Learn how to implement your persuasion techniques on all your social media websites and soon you will dominate your niche market.

Chapter 4

Lessons in Persuasion from the Top 5 Internet Marketing Gurus

The funny thing about tested persuasion techniques in online marketing is that they tend to work over and over again – no matter who uses them. This is why serious internet marketers form a tight knit community themselves and feed off each others good ideas. As an internet marketer you can learn a lot more from the great marketers of our time than from most 'how to' books.

That is why I have compiled a list of 5 of the very best. Each has made his fortune from persuasive marketing; each utilized it in a different way.

The Savvy Surfer: Frank Kern

Claim to Fame

 Frank Kern is the guy who has refined the art of mass control. He is a copywriting genius and uses mass persuasion to get leagues of people to buy, buy, buy! He has made a personal fortune of tens of millions of dollars through his selling techniques. As an online marketing guru he has successfully launched four businesses and made them a million dollars each in under one hour.

Because of his online success he has packaged his techniques and now sells them to others looking for a way to earn fast money online. The great thing is that people who buy these products are mostly impressed by him and say that they really do work.

Kern uses a form of persuasive control in language to invoke emotional responses in his potential clients. He uses words to draw the client in and establish a personal and immediate bond between them, making the potential sale a more realistic endeavor.

The biggest pitch that Kern sells is his claim that anyone can learn mass control techniques and use them without much effort at all.

Marketing Technique

Kern is a direct response specialist – he believes that building strong enduring relationships with his clients is the way to get them to buy his products. He takes this one step further and speaks about how to reach different clients in different formats – with music, video, images and writing.

He believes hard selling is an outdated and ineffectual form of selling and instead opts for a more seductive way of selling. Using friendly, honest coercion techniques Frank is able to sell anything he gets his hands on.

Kern teaches that the successful marketer uses the temporal relevance of the Internet to adapt and consistently improve upon their selling techniques. He asks his clients how to improve and then does it – giving them what they want. The result is a massive increase in sales revenue.

How You Can Implement It

Add email marketing to your list of priorities once your blog is up and running. Direct communication in Frank's opinion is pure gold. Your customers have chosen to hear more from you, now all you have to do is track their sales records or interests and market accordingly. Make sure that your emails aren't dry, intrusive or boring - people enjoy entertainment way more than hard selling!

The Internet Voyeur: John Reese

Claim to Fame

 John Reese was one of the first internet marketers ever; he began when the Internet did. Over the years he has earned millions and millions of dollars by carefully watching which internet trends work and what causes people to buy. He is a master at getting more people to your website and then converting them into buying customers.

As an internet marketer he was the first man to ever earn a million dollars in one day from online sales. He was also something of a pioneer with regards to auto responder services and the sales potential that they generate. Now of course he disagrees with them due to the rise of social media, personalization and direct selling.

Reese has also begun to teach others his tried and tested techniques of persuasive selling. He is an affiliate marketing advocate and firmly believes in passive income.

Marketing Technique

His main marketing technique involves driving the right traffic to an effective sales page. This involves working with affiliate programs, search engine optimization, pay per click marketing, Google Adword campaigns and studying search engine algorithms.

He is also a big fan of tracking results and re-launching sales sites to be more in line with what the buyers want and what they respond to best.

How You Can Implement It

If your website or blog has not been search engine optimized then its time for you to hire someone to do it. Look into the advertising market, investigate which affiliate programs you can enroll in and place on your blog. Start a Google Adwords campaign by bidding on targeted keywords to get your business ad placed on page one – this should drive more traffic to your website.

Use tracking programs like Google Analytics or stat Counter to see exactly what your potential clients are responding too – and change the ineffective material to something better.

The Viral Marketer: Mike Filsaime

Claim to Fame

 Mike Filsaime has a hand in many pies in the online marketing field, but he is best known for his incredible viral marketing abilities. As a man well versed in marketing offline he transferred his skills to the online arena several years ago with great success.

Creator of Butterfly Marketing – an intense and insightful viral marketing course that guides people through the process of promoting a new business online, Mike is a big believer in the interactivity of the Internet. He supports the concept that to sell products on your website you have to sell yourself.

Persuading people to buy your products or use your services because they like you is a brilliant concept. Unfortunately it's not so easy to implement – but that's where Mike comes in.

He has also been touring all over the country teaching people these principles of online sales. His sales page has a ton of satisfied customers bursting to tell you, the potential buyer, just how good his courses are. This is his way of convincing you to start convincing others.

Marketing Technique

Viral marketing is a form of word of mouth promotion whereby one client is so pleased or excited by your product or service that they feel compelled to let others know about it.

Filsaime is the king of viral marketing. He uses other people to convince buyers to buy. This method of advertising is very effective because of the group mentality that we spoke of earlier. A potential buyer online will almost always want to see what other people have said about a product before deciding to buy it.

His online techniques involve ethical selling, conversational/ personal business touches and always impressing the customer. With Mike around image and reputation is everything.

How You Can Implement It

Make sure that your business engages customers and treats them above the normal standard of service. Ask clients for honest reviews on your products and services so that you can post them on your business website, your blog and your social media sites.

Create hype for your business by using video, images and writing to encourage participation or comment from your potential clients. Friendly, down to earth, opinionated media always works.

Be entertaining – not everything on your blog or social media has to be about sales. Often the sites that sell the most are the sites that people enjoy visiting because they have sharp wit, something different to say or really outrageous opinions.

Post these insights and various media on Youtube, Facebook, Flickr – with unrestricted access and sharing of course!

The Straight Shooter: Dan Kennedy

Claim to Fame

As an internet marketer Dan Kennedy has a massive following. This is because he preaches the use of solid ethics and a no BS approach. People respond to his persuasive sales techniques because he knows how to prompt them to do so.

He believes that every successful online marketing campaign needs to be targeted at the right people, using the right media and with a pitch that is not only effective but downright irresistible.

Kennedy likes to help small business get off their feet and become self-empowered masters of their own sales destinies. He uses a very simple and logical method to attract buyers known as magnetic marketing. Ask the right questions and you'll get the right answers.

Marketing Technique

Kennedy is the father of online ethics. He believes in the old school straight-laced approach. If you want to sell something to someone give them a solid reason why they should buy it from you. When you fill in the why for the client you help them make up their mind.
Dan uses this persuasive selling technique to make millions for his clients. He now offers a wide range of courses that teaches marketers the language of selling online.

How You Can Implement It

Business ethics online are vitally important to your continued respect in the online arena. Tell the truth in your product descriptions, sales letters and promotional advertisements. People want the truth, not mutton dressed as lamb. Sales language can damage your business reputation – remember that hard selling rarely works.

The Real Authority: Brian Clark

Claim to Fame

When Brian Clark decided to become an authority in his niche market he took it to the next level. Now he is the owner of Copyblogger.com the Internet's main resource for people serious about learning how to blog, how to market online and write great copy.

Copyblogger is a few years old and yet it is one of the biggest blog sites on the internet. Clark has used his authority to sell products online and has become enormously successful in a very short space of time.

He has been called the king of the blogosphere because his blog posts on blogging are spread throughout social media repeatedly and people hang on his every instruction. This is mostly because he invites other online marketing authorities to blog on Copyblogger as well.

Marketing Technique

Brian uses wit, targeted action words and valuable information in his persuasive selling techniques. He is a master blogger and has connected with his potential clients on a whole other level. People who read his blog feel like they know Brian personally because he puts so much of himself into them.

How You Can Implement It

Work on establishing a unique and appealing voice on your business website and blog. Provide your client base with free valuable information about your niche market that they can't find anywhere else. Be an authority and dominate your market so that others approach you for guidance, links and advice.

Advice from the Masters

Each of these highly experienced internet marketers has something valuable to teach you. Use bits of advice from each of them or target one in particular that you think would be best for your industry. Mirroring the successful actions of someone else can often lead to conclusions of your own.

Whatever your decision as long as you are applying the main principles of online business persuasion, your online marketing campaign is sure to be launched in the right direction.

Chapter 5

Persuasive Selling: What You Need for Online Marketing Success

Persuasive Selling: The Road to Riches

There is more to being a persuasive seller than building a reputation and launching social media campaigns. Promotion is great to draw people to your website, but what happens once they've taken the hook and arrive on your landing page?

All that hard work has paid off and the client is looking through your website, reading the occasional product description or sales pitch – but what will convince them to take that final step and buy from you? You should make sure that every message on your website is persuasive or you could lose that sale.

Three Persuasive Business Practices

There are 3 definitive practices that you should employ if you want steady online business revenue. Many online marketers underestimate the power of these three elements and lose out on sales as a result. You don't want to make it any more difficult for yourself.

Clean Web Design

What is it about a simple, attractive, well planned website that keeps people coming back for more? It's easy to use, pleasant to look at and keeps its promises. Let's take a look at those three simple ideas.

Easy to Use – A successful website should have an uncomplicated navigation system that neatly orders its content in easily accessible places. There is a sitemap in case a potential client wants to find something fast. A business website should always be sharp, professional and informative.

Pleasant to Look at – There is a fine line between niche orientated imagery and a messy, crowded design. The graphics on your website should be attractive and simple, or at least arranged so that they don't detract from the sales content. First impressions often rely on your website design – so make it count by keeping things easy on the eye.

Promise Driven Website – What I mean by this is that the content is believable and the service delivery prompt, professional and timely. Your website could be the Mona Lisa of design with an incredible message – but if a client finds out those promises are empty – you will lose business.

Exceptional Customer Service

You have spent all this time building up your social networks and connecting with potential clients. The last thing you want to do is treat them like mindless sub human vessels once they take an interest in your products.

Make sure that you have a detailed FAQ page to answer questions that your business often receives. Thank your clients for their patronage by attaching a thank you note to their confirmation of sale email.

If you want to take that a step further include a few discount coupons on their next purchase. Reply immediately to clients who contact you directly with queries. You should also personalize your email replies – try auto attaching a personal email signature to each outgoing email.

If the customer sees the email is personally signed they feel special, appreciated and not like a faceless client receiving an auto business message. All of these actions show that you respect them as people and value them as clients. They will always come back for more if the service is good.

Choosing the Right Message

The old method of treating your clients like ignorant passers by is not going to work in your favor. Most of the people that come across your website are intelligent, and its better you understand that sooner rather than later. There is no 'stupid' client base that will fall for bad sales gimmicks, hollow tricks and seedy techniques.

If you try to manipulate, coerce or force your potential client to buy, they will recognize what you are trying to do and reject you, your business and any pitches of yours that they come across at a later date. Using business persuasion is not about skipping through the hard work and tricking your clients into buying.

Hard selling is becoming incredibly unpopular – even those long form sales letters we see all over the Internet are becoming redundant. People don't want long winded, hyped up nonsense. They want you to treat them with respect. They want honesty, integrity and a direct message that is not only true, but affirmed by the rest of your client base.

Don't give them a reason to dislike you. Monitor your client's movements and needs and give them what they want – it can only help you in the end.

Tips for Writing and Advertising

Knowing which specific writing and advertising techniques to use on your website and blog can make all the difference in your persuasive selling campaign. People respond to certain formulas and they can be a massive boost to your selling skills.

Persuasive Writing Techniques

For every kind of writing there is a structure. They all have three things in common, and that is that they should all have a catchy headline, a good reason to buy and the benefits of buying such an item or service.

Address Your Potential Client

In any persuasive selling it's always best to directly address your potential client and to answer the questions that cast doubt in their minds as to whether or not they should buy something. Detail exactly what they will receive if they decide to buy the product – make the pitch more about them and less about the product itself.

Don't Be Afraid to Sell

If you don't directly offer them the product, then it might as well be a catalogue description in a library book. You are trying to get your client to accept your product or service as something that they need or want enough to buy. Psychologically if your pitch is sincere and honest the 'buy now' at the end can be very effective.

Say it Again

One of the most tested sales techniques is repeating your sales pitch to your client. Repetition is about getting the client to understand your persuasive argument by presenting it in different ways in the same content. By covering all possible angles you ensure that the client knows exactly what you are saying. People are more likely to buy if you make the educated decision for them.

Be Consistent

Writing is all about delivering a quality, well thought out message to the reader. In sales we want the reader to take action. In order to achieve this we need to be consistent in our approach from start to finish.

If you have a sales letter that starts off well, has an amazing middle and a sloppy ending - it doesn't bode well with the client. Subconsciously they will find this attempt lacking and perceive your business the same way.

The same goes for all of your writing. Keep the level of persuasion and quality high so that clients notice your consistency instead of rejecting it.

Use the English Language

Relating a product to a personal story can take you far in a sales pitch, especially when you know how to use the English language to express your point and support your argument. Getting an emotional response from your potential client will almost always have a favorable consequence.

This is why metaphors, analogies, strong alliterations and comparisons can make a pitch work so well. Use English to your advantage, but be careful of too much flourish in your words, it will only drive your clients away.

The Power of Questions

 Asking and then answering questions is an excellent way of clearing the path to a sale. If you stress how difficult the question is for example, and cause the client a bit of anxiety – then solve it swiftly further down – you will invoke feelings of gratitude and a need for the same solution. If that solution is your product then you've won.

Be careful when using this technique, if the question comes across as fabricated or if you blow it way out of proportion it will ruin your solution. For example you sell toothbrushes and have written a sales letter explaining how without this toothbrush your client's teeth are going to rot and fall out. Your client knows this won't happen and will dismiss your entire pitch as a pack of lies.

Sales Stereotyping

More than anything people want to be part of something. If you can offer them a way to be part of a desired social group then they will buy your product. Playing on exclusivity, wealth and popularity may at times seem fickle, but this persuasive technique has lasted – and for good reason.

Use a convincing sales pitch to associate your potential client with that exclusive group, whoever they may be, and then explain how your product will make them the envy of that social group. If you present a good argument with all of the previous features of a good persuasive online marketing campaign – you will sell.

Persuasive Advertising Techniques

Suggestive advertising is always a challenge, but it is a fundamental part of your persuasive marketing campaign. Banner ads, viral marketing ads and promotional content on your social media pages all form the crux of your advertising reach.

There are 2 specific persuasive advertising techniques that you should familiarize yourself with that will lead to increased sales conversions.

Give People Free Stuff

Marketers always underestimate this one, to their detriment. Giving people free products, special offers and exclusive downloads builds trust and loyalty between you and your clients. Plus it can act as a free advertising tool for you as well.

Offering free e-books on your website on informative subjects and then relating them to your products or including your links/brand, can spread the word about the generosity of your business. It will also establish you as an authority.

Couple your products together in a buy one, get another free kind of package. Offer discounts off your other products when purchasing one specific kind – be creative and offer free stuff of actual quality.

Humor Sells

Most people online are there to be entertained. People would much rather watch a funny Youtube video than read your long winded sales pitch. If you can capture their attention with wit and humor then you are well on your way to selling big.

This is key for short texts like adverts. People are so used to seeing flashing banners and fancy graphics that they hardly give them more than a passing glance. If you can attract them with graphics and then hook them with wit or humor - then they will click forward to your sales pages.

Ineffective Sales Techniques

Do Not:

- Explain the obvious to your clients
- Put your product down or excuse it because you are afraid it is inferior
- Be demanding or make passive threats
- Announce how honest you are and how everyone else is not
- Talk excessively about yourself – its about your client
- Forget about calls to action – you need them or people won't act
- Create impersonal auto response relationships
- Be too formal – everything online is about conversational writing
- Include irrelevant information
- Misuse punctuation to make your point or overuse color, bold or underlining

Integrating the correct persuasive writing into your online marketing techniques can do wonders for your business message. Once you have realized that your business needs to entertain and well as educate in order to sell – then you will be on your way to effective selling.

Promotion is only as good as the message you use once you've driven people to your website. If your website is cluttered and your writing boring and unclear nobody is going to buy your products.

This is why setting the correct climate is so important when selling – if a client isn't in the right buying mood, or has doubts about your business – chances are they are just going to pass through. Make sure that you never give them such an easy reason to leave.

Chapter 6

How to Create the Perfect Online Sales Climate

Setting the Perfect Sales Climate

The astute internet marketer knows that buying is an emotional response to certain factors created by the seller. When selling online you are among an endless list of alternatives, and this is where most amateur businesses come up short.

On this highly competitive platform it would be unwise to believe that your products will sell as long as they are visible. This is not true. Having excellent search engine rankings and an amazing advertising or social media campaign can only get people to your website – and that's when the real battle begins.

So far all you have done is persuaded your potential client to click on a link or an advert. It is a wholly different set of responses that will persuade them to take that massive leap and actually buy from you.

You've got a curious potential buyer on your website – what factors will aid them in making that crucial decision to buy from you?

The Perfect Website

Having a website that is not only inviting to your clients but stimulates their need to buy is simple enough. The challenge is to perfect your niche market formula. Depending on your business and the products or services that you provide, you will make decisions as to the layout, content and extras that go into making it the ideal sales climate for potential buyers.

Only you know what your target market is – if no particular design comes to mind then check out the competition for ideas and improve upon them. Here are some basic features that you should consider when building a business website

Niche Graphics

Clean, simple and attractive graphics can work for any business website regardless of niche. People often get carried away and use graphics that are overly complicated, too prominent or force the rest of the site to have an illogical navigation system.

Your website is live all day everyday – you need to focus on professional, simple graphics so that it communicates the right message to your clients on their first visit. This said; do not fall into the template trap.

Some template websites can be customized but if you launch a website that looks and functions like 100 others online people may notice and regard you as a temporary trader in it for a quick buck. Your website graphics are an excellent investment; make sure that yours are done right.

Logical Content Division

Grouping products together and making sure that they are easily searchable on your businesses search tool can be the difference between a sale and a frustrated visitor leaving your site for greener pastures.

Make sure that your products/services are divided into the right sections of your website, that they have a logical page content flow and that each product is 'filed' properly. Imagine a news report being filed under e-books for sale – the only people who are going to buy it are impulse shoppers' not targeted searchers.

Targeting Marketing Success

Every decision that you make on your website should be geared toward selling something effectively to your client. If it doesn't then leave it out. Your website is not a personal chalk board for useless information – every piece of it needs to be carefully crafted for marketing success.

Use persuasive language techniques in your content, be friendly, and offer free advice or free downloads to establish trust, all of your persuasion skills need to be used on your website.

Most sales websites online are not geared toward this ultimate goal. This is because their owners do not acknowledge the emotional side of sales. Their wares are posted haphazardly and left on a blank surface – but they are communicating the wrong message.

A cold, clinical and unfriendly website will drive most visitors away. There is no persuasion involved. This is why creating that perfect emotional climate is so vital. Use what you have learnt in this book to help create a client centered website that connects with them emotionally and watch the sales pour in.

The Next Step

How do you expand upon that perfect sales climate after your website launch? Once you have started selling and accumulating clients the next step is to keep in contact with them. You are at an advantage here because you know that they are willing to buy from your business. They know that they receive quality of service and that you keep your promises.

This kind of client is ripe for repeat business. Half of your battle is won; you have broken through that barrier and can now begin to nurture a repeat sales relationship with them – but how?

RSS Feed Basics

An RSS feed will continue to keep your client informed about what is happening with your business. Your really simple syndication feed (RSS) should be attached to your blog and linked to your business website.

Encouraging clients to follow your RSS feed in your sales confirmation letter will add new dimensions to your business/client relationship. Your RSS feed will give them a way to read all updated content on your site in one place.

This means if you have important announcements, special sales coming up, competitions running or new blog entries – all of these will be accessible to your client at the click of a button.

Remember that in order for this to work effectively you have to create a personality behind your business. If you are selling boring mundane objects, very few people will want to be constantly updated on them, unless you are really entertaining to read.

Pimp Your Feed

You can make your RSS feed indispensable to people in your own industry by inviting guest authorities to write for your blog. By having all the latest news, issues and debates in one place you add to your reputation and will get more people following your feed.

It acts as a unique marketing tool because it draws people back to your website or blog where they can then be exposed to your sales techniques again. RSS feeds are a major asset to your business because they're an ongoing source of advertising for free.

Secrets of Direct Email Marketing

When it comes to repeat business few marketing techniques are as effective as direct email marketing. The problem is that people rarely know how to use this efficient medium to their advantage.

Email marketing campaigns can go horribly wrong and can even ruin your business if they aren't properly handled. Here are a few iron clad techniques to ensure that your clients keep coming back for more.

To Spam or not to Spam?

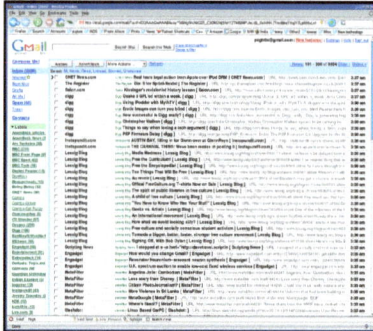

There are some businesses online today that have the misguided opinion that virtually papering their clients inboxes with special offers and information will get them repeat sales. It won't, and more and more marketers are discovering this the hard way.

Spamming your clients is never the answer, and it will make them regret ever buying anything from you. This is not the best frame of mind for them to have especially when you want to keep them as paying customers.

Think of your clients as you think of your business - professional, intelligent and willing to hear a genuinely beneficial sales pitch for a relative item. You have to decide that enough is enough and send a maximum of one, maybe two emails to your clients every month.

One well-written, friendly, relevant email can do far more than fifteen emails of a lower caliber.

Targeted Email Marketing

You are able to monitor the movements and sales on your website thanks to analytics programs that record important marketing data for you. Use this advantage to compile unique profiles for your clients, tracking what they buy, what they look at and are interested in and how much they are willing to spend online.

Then use this to create a targeted email especially for that one client. Tempt them with relevant items that they may truly want and you'll be amazed at how often people will respond.

The email to sale conversion rate is far higher because you are taking more time to get to know your clients. They will see this and be glad to read your offers because they are interesting and tailored to their needs. Most businesses can't be bothered doing this, even though there are programs who do all of the work for you.

Be proactive about getting sales and 1000 could easily become 100,000. Send your emails out on a Tuesday or Wednesday, people tend to make decisions and are most productive and alert then.

Beating Spam Filters

Even though you have your clients email address and have created a great targeted email for them, the mail may never be read. To avoid wasting your time eliminate hard selling and clichéd sales language from your subject line.

A simple way of beating spam filters is by addressing the client by name. This will ensure that it doesn't end up in the junk mail box only to be auto deleted.

Keep it Clear, Short and Simple

Make sure that by the first sentence of your email the client knows what you want from them. By keeping the email short you prevent a 5 minute loading time that will cause most people to close the email and never read it again. Most people will wait 5 seconds, any more than that and you are lucky they bothered.

Use attractive images in your pitch, but remember to be conversational and friendly. People very rarely respond to a sales onslaught of 100 products for sale, tailored or not. Keep it down to two or three maximum and definitely not all in images.

Template emails may be easier but they are ineffective so there is no good reason to use them. There is such a thing as overkill, so try to prevent any of that creeping into your emails even if offer 52 is the best one yet. Remember less is more.

How Do You Set Up Your Own Email Marketing Campaign?

Get a Good Auto Responder Like Aweber – You can load your targeted emails onto this service and it will send them at your specified date and time. Sign up and use the service – it's that simple.

Targeted Email Template – Not a template email but a template with your basic email structure that you will customize later.

Build a Client List – Establish a sign-up option on your blog and business website's landing page. This will give your clients the opportunity to receive your marketing updates.

Don't forget to always include a friendly but firm call to action in each email. Creating the perfect online sales climate is a lot of hard work but the rewards are evident soon after you start.

The key to successful online business persuasion is setting the tone, and then getting the rest right. Without a great website and a means to create repeat business, your marketing campaign will crumble. Build your businesses community and nurture it to get the most out of your efforts.

Chapter 7

Killing the Competition: Credibility, Believability and Likeability

Being a Strong Competitor

In order for you to become a top notch internet marketer you need to constantly remind yourself that you are a competitor in the fiercest marketing arena ever created. People lose sight of this because they don't have to be in direct contact with the competition.

This doesn't mean that they aren't watching your every move and carefully making their own business decisions to overshadow yours. If you are losing sales it's because there are other companies out there who are getting them. There is no such thing as a shortage of clientele online. They are buying from somebody else.

Being a strong competitor online will draw people to your sales website and earn you money. Your first step after launching your website and your various promotional campaigns is to gain client trust.

This can be achieved using the persuasive techniques of credibility, believability and likeability. If you perfect these facets of your service portfolio then finding clients will never be an issue for your business.

Creating a Credible Online Image

Making sure that your business appears credible online will not only boost your sales but help your search engine ranking as well. It may seem easy enough to achieve, but in fact its one of the most difficult and intangible images to portray. This is because your clients have to decide to do business with you based on face value.

They have never met you. They only know what your website tells them. They have no idea whether buying from you will be a wise decision for them to make. Building credibility online will help your believability and likeability factors too, so it's important to work on these immediately after your website is designed.

The important thing here is to eliminate any thoughts in your visitors minds that they are going to encounter dishonesty, manipulation or bad service while on your website.

Establishing credibility is the beginning of your career long struggle for a perfect reputation. It doesn't happen overnight, but you can make sure that all of your business practices are trustworthy so that it eventually does happen.

There is no point in being deceitful because the Internet is like a glass door. Everyone will see how untrustworthy you are and eventually shut you down. The only businesses that survive are the ones who are doing something right. There are no short cuts here – be trustworthy and the world will see it.

Credibility involves your business practices, how you project the image of your business and how you interact with clients. All of this contributes to making your business approachable, usable and credible.

For a Credible Business Image

Include all business details on your website like address, phone number and links to other relevant sites. If you can, show what business you have already done, or testimonials proving that you are trustworthy.

Authenticate your business by adding photos of your offices, staff and staff get-togethers to your website. It will add a friendly face to your sales pitches and that emotional human element that potential buyers like to connect with.

Use as many awards, citations, references and outgoing links to other credible affiliate sites as you can.

Be lighting fast when answering client queries. If the question has already been answered on your FAQ page then send them the link. Other than that most other queries should be handled individually. Auto replies only alienate your client.

Make sure that all the relevant security measures are put in place to protect your clients – and place them in a convenient location so that they are visible to visitors. Privacy policies and credit security are major concerns; make sure that your clients know their private information won't go awry.

How to Earn From Believability

Believability is the product of credibility. When your clients trust you they are more open to your sales pitches and more willing to spend time on your website taking in all of the details.

At this point you can get previously satisfied clients to write testimonials for you to encourage new potential clients to buy. You can also work on reviews that your clients can endorse, or get them to write up a simple review themselves.

Often when a client receives service that is above and beyond the norm, they are only too happy to help.

Ask Yourself These Questions:

Are your sales pitches believable? Are they honest or have they been laced with false promises? Are your images the real product images or stock internet database images? Have you asked clients how to produce a better service for them

All of these questions will help you attach more believability to your website, blog and social media pages.

You must maintain a professional, helpful and trustworthy reputation. It's difficult to create and easy to lose. Remember that the more business you create, the more business you will receive. This is because people are more likely to believe numbers than words. If you are a multi-million dollar company that has earned 10 million dollars – chances are your product is amazing and you are telling the truth in your sales pitches.

Ethics are important to believability, so is consistency. If there are mixed reviews about your products or services out there, most people will view that as a negative and take their business elsewhere.

Giving free stuff away can help you build an instant relationship with a potential client. It will make them more likely to believe that you put your customers first. You don't want to look like you are only in it for the money, but that you are also in it for the satisfaction/pride of being the best.

Try and steer clear of sales language, make your product descriptions exciting and add personality to your website. It will only help establish your business as an emotional entity in a sea of clinical, uncaring alternatives.

Turn specific results, data, or numbers into believable stats that you willingly share with your clients. For example, in August of 2013 our top selling product was X, exploding onto the market and breaking our product record of $2,645. Help us better it this month!

Instill in your clients the confidence to buy from you, knowing that they are getting the better deal and the best service from a business that cares.

Likeability: How Being Liked Can Make You a Millionaire

Experienced internet marketers will tell you that being likable is the key to everything. It's more important than excellent business service, great products or streams of testimonials.

If you succeed at making your business likable, then you are on the path to riches. When it comes to persuasion in online marketing, there are simple principles that you need to understand in order make your business a success. Who in your life are you most likely to trust? The answer is the people around you who you most care about.

This same principle applied online can make you a millionaire. If you interact enough with your client base, then the sky is the limit for your earning potential. Connecting and allowing yourself to get professionally involved with your clients via your blog or social media will guarantee that they use your services, or buy your products, every time.

Establishing a business based friendship with your clients all but guarantees online success. It is the one element that allows small business to compete with the corporations who dominate the offline world.

Here are some key features that you need to apply to your business practices in order to make it big:

Availability

People notice when a business treats them with individual respect, and replies to all of their queries and suggestions. Making yourself and your staff members available for online interaction is a great way to establish those coveted business bonds. The Internet is the only arena where you can communicate with your clients real-time. Use it to your advantage and soon you'll have a league of loyal fans.

Be Positive

It is so important to emit a positive tone when writing about your business or trying to sell something to a client. No one wants to drown in misery, sarcasm or dreary sales talk that the writer himself hardly believes in. By being positive you can help your clients' associate energy, hard work, professionalism, vibrancy and effectiveness with your business.

Personalization

Treating your clients as individuals cannot be stressed enough. If you send them an email addressed impersonally then they won't mind deleting it. If you address the email to them directly using their names and perhaps relating to a conversation that you had before, then they will sit up and take notice. That's just good business.

Humor

Everyone likes to be entertained. In fact statistics show that there are more people online who are interested in entertainment than anything else. This isn't surprising. What is surprising is that there are still many internet marketers who don't include humor, light hearted wit or entertainment in their campaigns. Give people what they want by being entertaining.

This comes into play with the personality that you give your business. Whatever the tone, you should always include wit and humor in whatever you write. People are more likely to like you if you have something entertaining to say.

Firm Belief in Your Business

Believe in the business practices you have laid out for your business and don't second-guess yourself. Because of the client interaction on your blogs and social media you are sure to come across criticism or complaints.

Use these platforms to professionally handle the problem and straighten things out. Always side with your policies – remember that believing in your business encourages others to do so as well.

Using the Secrets of Online Business Persuasion

Now that you have discovered the secrets to business persuasion online, there must be a lot of new ideas swirling around your mind, bursting to be implemented. These techniques can take you all the way if you concentrate on executing each and every one. They all work together to form the ultimate sales persuasion for any part of the collective whole.

The best piece of advice anyone can give you when you are set on becoming the next Frank Kern or Mike Filsaime, is to keep up to date on current internet marketing trends. Continuous research, study and application will help you keep ahead of your competitors. Remember that 'interaction' is the name of the internet marketing game. Now get out there and apply these techniques to your online marketing campaign and see how well they work for you.

Let's Recap What You've Learnt:

- **Your online marketing skills can always be improved**
- Persuasion can be applied to every facet of your campaign
- **You can use virtual crowd psychology to influence the collective whole**
- You must establish yourself as a market leader and build your brand identity
- **Eliminate your potential clients reasons not to buy from you**
- Launch a social media campaign to promote your business website
- **Use your Blog, Facebook page and Twitter account to build an online community**
- Learn and apply persuasive sales techniques from the worlds best internet marketers
- **Apply persuasive selling to your website content and all other writing and advertising media**
- Set the perfect sales climate by creating the right website, and using your RSS feed and email marketing campaign as a source of repeat revenue
- **Build credibility, believability and likeability for your business to continuously draw new sales and sustain repeat relationships**
- Use what you have learnt in this book to dominate your market

www.ingramcontent.com/pod-product-compliance
Lightning Source LLC
Chambersburg PA
CBHW051103180526
45172CB00002B/760